THIS BOOK BELENDER TO:

○ — — — — — — — — — — — — — — ○

○ — — — — — — — — — — — — — — ○

Each page is filled with fun things to discover don't forget to color them in for even more creativity! Enjoy finding the hidden items and use your imagination to bring each picture to life and make it even more **fun !**

Author

Oliver West

I SPY WITH MY LITTLE EYE
SOMETHING BEGINNING WITH...

I SPY WITH MY LITTLE EYE SOMETHING BEGINNING WITH...

C

IS FOR

CAT

I SPY WITH MY LITTLE EYE SOMETHING BEGINNING WITH...

I SPY WITH MY LITTLE EYE
SOMETHING BEGINNING WITH...

D

IS FOR

DRAGON

I SPY WITH MY LITTLE EYE
SOMETHING BEGINNING WITH...

I SPY WITH MY LITTLE EYE SOMETHING BEGINNING WITH...

G

I SPY WITH MY LITTLE EYE SOMETHING BEGINNING WITH...

I SPY WITH MY LITTLE EYE SOMETHING BEGINNING WITH...

H

IS FOR

HAT

I SPY WITH MY LITTLE EYE SOMETHING BEGINNING WITH...

I SPY WITH MY LITTLE EYE SOMETHING BEGINNING WITH...

IS FOR

ICE CREAM

I SPY WITH MY LITTLE EYE
SOMETHING BEGINNING WITH...

I SPY WITH MY LITTLE EYE SOMETHING BEGINNING WITH...

M

IS FOR

MOUSE

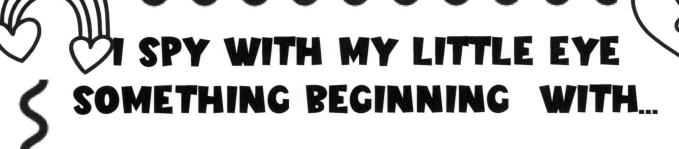

I SPY WITH MY LITTLE EYE SOMETHING BEGINNING WITH...

IS FOR

NOTEBOOK

I SPY WITH MY LITTLE EYE SOMETHING BEGINNING WITH...

I SPY WITH MY LITTLE EYE SOMETHING BEGINNING WITH...

P

IS FOR

PUMPKIN

I SPY WITH MY LITTLE EYE
SOMETHING BEGINNING WITH...

Q

I SPY WITH MY LITTLE EYE SOMETHING BEGINNING WITH...

Q

IS FOR

QUEEN

I SPY WITH MY LITTLE EYE SOMETHING BEGINNING WITH...

I SPY WITH MY LITTLE EYE SOMETHING BEGINNING WITH...

S

IS FOR

STRAWBERRY

I SPY WITH MY LITTLE EYE SOMETHING BEGINNING WITH...

I SPY WITH MY LITTLE EYE SOMETHING BEGINNING WITH...

I SPY WITH MY LITTLE EYE
SOMETHING BEGINNING WITH...

W

I SPY WITH MY LITTLE EYE SOMETHING BEGINNING WITH...

I SPY WITH MY LITTLE EYE
SOMETHING BEGINNING WITH...

Made in United States
Orlando, FL
04 January 2025

56890161R00030